The Maker of Glass Eyes

BOB MEE

Cinnamon Press

Published by Cinnamon Press
Meirion House
Glan yr afon
Tanygrisiau
Blaenau Ffestiniog
Gwynedd
LL41 3SU
www.cinnamonpress.com

The right of Bob Mee to be identified as author of this work has been asserted by him in accordance with the Copyright, Designs and Patent Act, 1988. Copyright © 2009 Bob Mee
ISBN: 978-1-905614-82-0
British Library Cataloguing in Publication Data. A CIP record for this book can be obtained from the British Library.

All rights reserved. No part of this publication may be reproduced, stored in a retrieval system, or transmitted in any form or by any means, electronic, mechanical, photocopying, recording or otherwise without either the prior written permission of the publishers. This book may not be lent, hired out, resold or otherwise disposed of by way of trade in any form of binding or cover other than that in which it is published, without the prior consent of the publishers.

Designed and typeset in Palatino by Cinnamon Press. Cover design by Mike Fortune-Wood from original artwork by Bob Mee, used with kind permission.

Printed in Great Britain by the MPG Books Group,
Bodmin and King's Lynn

Acknowledgements

Thanks are due to the editors of the following publications in which some of the poems, some in different forms, first appeared: *Envoi*, the *Essex Poetry Competition pamphlet* and *Poetry Monthly*.

Contents

1959	9
Strict and Particular Baptist	10
The Red Tablecloth	11
Unidentified	12
An Excerpt from the Sequence Millicent Martin in Garmisch-Partenkirchen	13
The Maker of Glass Eyes	14
Baldy Head	16
The Sisters	20
Gustav Mahler in Toronto	22
Nelson and Hardy Play Scrabble Before Trafalgar	24
The Bet	25
The Water Diviner	26
Des	27
Wood	28
Fishing with Jack	29
Test Paper	30
Holding the Days	31
Ellyn, Stratford Pool	32
Campsite	33
On the Famous Photograph of Stanley Matthews on Mount Everest	34
The Gallery of Goalkeepers	36
Elizabeth Barrett Browning's Lost Years	38
Mr and Mrs Shakespeare in a Café in Rother Street	40
Camping, Northern Spain	41
Before	42
Vigil	44
Stranded	46
A Hat	48
A Giant	49

Not Leaving	50
Beach Cricket	51
Walking Across the Mersey	52
Grief	54
Rain	55
Where Things Go	56
Early Morning, Herefordshire	57
Of Gambling and Poetry	58
The Open Mic Poetry Reading	60
Las Vegas, 6.15 a.m.	62
In the Hotel Room Next to the Mountain	64
Clearing the Boundaries of the Revolution	66
The Ice	67
House of Fun	70
Dreaming on the Broken Boulevard	71
Utopia, California, 1999	72
Ericsson the Engineer in Marshalsea Jail	74
The Guardians of the Lady's Slipper Orchid	75
The Release of the First Starlings in America	76
Wall	78
Aunt Mary	80

The Maker of Glass Eyes

1959

I'm on a train with my father going to see my aunt.
My father's smoked too many Woodbines and slumps
in the corner of the Third Class compartment.
He's pulled his cap down tight, hunched his shoulders deep inside
his raincoat. By the window, I smell the coal from the engine,
watch wet fields and small towns.

When we get off my father will be sick into a litter bin
and the station master will shout at us
and my father will dab his mouth with a hankie as we walk away.
I'll reach up and hold his hand. His eyes bloodshot, watery.
I won't remember what we'll say.

My father and I will visit my blind aunt
just out of hospital after trapping her finger-ends in a door.
I will remember the large yews in the grounds,
our feet on the gravel drive; inside the dark green room
my aunt trying to knit with one hand.

All that's in the future, of course.
For now I am on the train as it drifts between quiet stations
and the fields and towns of Northamptonshire,
my father's face yellow as his fingers.

Strict and Particular Baptist

Wasps in jam jars of runny jelly on the windowsill by the door to
the damp orchard. I sat on the seat to read and got a wet behind.

Luther, remember, Luther, as the thunder rumbles. The just
shall live by the faith. Romans One, Seventeen.

Tea's ready, dear. And his footsteps steady across the study,
descending the stairs.

And the framed photograph of her on the sideboard, hairstyle
just the same. Oh, she was so very young.

White railings by the brook. I ran my hands along them on the way
from the bus. Sunday School at three, Evening Service at six.

Elbows off the table, Robert! Carnation milk, tinned fruit.
Cherries that glowed. Is this pineapple? I like this!

Windows open, the sound of pigeons in the deep green trees,
the clinking of spoons and stirring of sugar lumps into weak tea.

A mark of grace is humility. The Lord enabled Handel to compose
The Messiah in twenty-two days.

And my father all in white immersed in the name of the Father
and the Son and the Holy Ghost.

And in the pulpit ad-libbed sermons lasting forty minutes, a bellowing
of faith and certainty. Why was the top of his finger missing?

The last bus at a quarter to eight. Or the occasional lift home
in the Lanchester, and guilty for it. Dad sucking on a sprig of privet.

The Red Tablecloth

I sit under the red tablecloth and the table that's old as father. I have just started school.

I stay here a long time. There are red times, brown times and a time not quite black.

I peep out, smell fresh-mown grass in new rain. *It's only a shower*, says my blind aunt, who turns and stares above my head: *Even you, little boy, must ask forgiveness in Jesus' name.*

Under the red tablecloth my beautiful baby brother sleeps. He is already growing up. Soon we shall play together.

Under the red tablecloth it is bedtime. My mother smooths my hair, pats the eiderdown, her breath peppermints, fear.

Now I am eight, going on nine. My bedroom door is open and downstairs in the kitchen, father talks to mother. He talks for a long time. I feel mother shuddering as she bows her head.

Under the red tablecloth I hear our visitors agree the time limit for appropriate grief is one year. They call each other Mr, Mrs and Miss and I hear the phrase, *a just and merciful God*. Mother has set out the good cups from the top shelf. My blind aunt turns hers over, feels its weight, runs a finger along its rim.

Under the red tablecloth I still say to my brother: *Wake up, it's not Sunday, we can go out to play*. From heaven, he hugs me.

Unidentified

Our family tree is meticulously detailed. We can go back four centuries. No missing links. No strays.

But in the Asda checkout queue I see my mother. Dead ten years, there she is in her red coat, the good one she kept for best. The same short dark perm, the crown of her head in the same place, bone structure, weight, smile, eyes.

I know she'll prefer tea to coffee, take no sugar; will have left school too soon but will be proud of her prize for spelling chrysanthemum. She will adore children.

Too far ahead, she's gone before I can call out. I leave the trolley, push through with excuse-mes and sorrys.

Too late.

I stand in the rain, wonder what to do.

An Excerpt from the Sequence Millicent Martin in Garmisch-Partenkirchen

...one, that one there,
with the strappy maroon dress and bare arms
is remembering how scared she was
waiting for the last train to Lincoln
when a monk lay on a bench
sucking his thumb
watching her.
As she left she heard him say
My Angel!

Now she's smiling as the host
who has something
of the monk about him
loudly tells a joke
and she hands on
the dish of artichokes
to her fashionable husband
who is not one of
her passions.

Her husband mentions Juke Box Jury
and people shout out names
David Jacobs... Pete Murray...
Nancy Spain... Millicent Martin

Oh yes, says the girl who incidentally
has her hair in a pony-tail
and has a bullet scar on her left temple,
I met Millicent Martin in Garmisch-Partenkirchen.
The skiing is good there and the lake is lovely...

The Maker of Glass Eyes

My customers come at night. I hear
their tap-tap upon the cobbles, wait
to assess the character of their knock
upon my heavy door. In order to match
precise colour and tone I ask them
to lie back in my reclining chair, a
present from my mother, from whom I
have inherited my sense of discipline and
control. Some are startled by vulnerability,
others made uneasy by direct light in their
one good eye. One or two murmur prayers.
All, eventually, offer up their secrets.
I am discreet as a priest.

Of course, there are evenings when
the terrifying possibility of conversation
outweighs the dull necessity of income.
Then in the shelter of my wood-panelled room
I do not answer the raps of the gloved knuckles,
do not move when they are repeated, increase
in urgency. The most persistent or desperate
lean close and call out my name, softly, as if
fearful of discovery. I feel their breath.

In the mornings I begin work early, take
comfort in the babble and song of the woman
and children next door, in the bustle of
the perpetually damp courtyard. I arrange
my eyes tray by labelled tray upon the oak
table, a present from my father, from whom
I have inherited my unusual countenance
and attention to detail. My eyes are numbered
and named. I like to fancy if they met
in the street, they would recognise each
other, perhaps exchange a sly wink.

The wearer of each gleaming celebration
of my craftsmanship will no longer be
the person they were. With my tiny brushes,
I create personal histories in layers. I build
misery and shame in a network of capillaries,
add on joy, cunning and lust in the subtle
blends of the brown and blue iris, and
last of all, in the slightly dilated pupil,
the ability to lie and deceive.

Baldy Head

I. The Man

The kids in the street laughed and chanted *Baldy Head, Baldy Head!*
It was my wife's fault. An old recipe of her grandmother's, she said.
Rub goose grease into the scalp before you go to bed, she said.
In the morning on the pillow there was a clump of something
greasy and congealed like a drowned hamster. Matted hair.
And where I'd rolled over it was laid out like grass
peeled loose from the tyres of a lawn-mower.
All that was left was my eyebrows.

I bought the best shampoo to keep them soft and silky
as a Labrador's ears.

II. The Woman

Yes, we had a row, a stormer.
He said I'd been in the bath so long I could have rowed
across the North Sea in it and had breakfast in Ostend.
I laughed, said *Good job it doesn't float then*.
He thundered his fists on the door.
I sank under the water to hide. When I came out
he was drinking at the kitchen table, drawing mad diagrams
on sheets of foolscap. Dozens were screwed up on the floor.
He had out the box of sea-faring instruments he bought
at auction last summer, was muttering:
It can be done. It can be done.

By morning, he'd gone.

III. The Coastguard

We got the call at three-thirty, a cock-eyed tale of a mayday flare
from a man rowing a bath across the North Sea.
We blamed it on a bad line. We didn't know what to look for,
flew as close to the waves as the gale would allow.
Nobody lasts more than an hour out there
and we made one last sweep and saw something
shining in the searchlight like a huge coin in the water:
It was his bald head.

Bill went down and we winched him up. He lay on the floor
clutching an expensive bottle of shampoo by Vidal Sassoon.
The forms had to be filled in so I asked him how he thought
he might have got into difficulties. *Ah*, he said, lifting
himself on to one elbow. *It was when the waves
started coming in over the side. I thought the quickest way
to get the water out was to pull out the plug.*

IV. The Man

My wife, whose hair is sprouting like a spider plant,
just goes on handing out the tablets.
I sit in my dressing gown and slippers
and watch rain running down windows.
Perhaps there'll be a flood: streets will become rivers,
mountains lakes, and perhaps, maybe, all the baths
in the city will take to the water. In every one
men with lunch appointments in Ostend
will clutch lap-tops and umbrellas.
And on the quayside chauffeurs will hold up
placards with names written boldly
but slightly mis-spelled
in a skew-wiff felt tip.

When I get over-excited she distracts me
with the ten thousand piece jigsaw on the construction
of the Kon Tiki—Thor Heyerdahl,
he was bald too you know, really, he was.

I have to finish it between meal-times
or it gets cleared away.

I always begin with the sea.

The Sisters

They floated past on the icy road in their noiseless cars.
In the old days we would have waved small paper flags and cheered.
This time we stared.
Even so, I like to think I caught the duke's eye.
We craned our necks to watch them wind up the mountain road.
As we walked home, linking arms, the first snows fell.
We were laughing with exhilaration.

In the cafe we heard such scandalous things.
We have never, as they say, swung the bat
for one side or another, except for my sister's
brief dalliance with the son of the cardinal,
but that was many years ago.
So much ego, my sister, all drama and no plot.

How people talk!
Why was the old queen wearing sunglasses?
Did you see the royal dogs had a car to themselves?
The youngest prince is an alcoholic, you know.
His own father barely tolerates him.
And they say his wife has a merkin made of diamonds.
I spat out my coffee at that.
The old woman who'd said it laughed at me.
Don't worry, my dear, no doubt it's washed regularly.

A ragged boy ran in, breathless.
An accident, he said, in the mountains.
We all ran down to the low bridge, pulling on
our winter coats as we went.
My sister and I wedged ourselves between a priest
and the blacksmith's half-wit daughter, who was giggling
and bobbing up and down.

The partisans brought them through in an open truck.
As it clattered across the bridge, I saw the bodies jumbled
together, bouncing. Blood trickling from an ear,
an arm flung out in salute or surrender,
the duke's blue eyes glaring.

Gustav Mahler in Toronto

He sips an Espresso in a dark corner of the bar,
burrows in behind the collar of his overcoat.
He has a Blue Jays baseball cap pulled tight
but I recognise his famously broken nose.
tortoise-shell spectacles and the way
a tuft of wire-grey hair escapes above his ears.

His hands shake as he grips the cup.
He says to me: *Why are they painting my name all over town?*
And it's true. Wherever you go, it's there.
Splashed in red paint on the sides of bridges GUSTAV MAHLER.
On the tops of buses GUSTAV MAHLER.
Even on the wall of the city's main police station GUSTAV MAHLER.
When the Toronto Argonauts run out into the stadium
they see

```
            G                   G
            U                   U
            S                   S
            T                   T
            A  GUSTAV MAHLER    A
            V                   V
            M                   M
            A                   A
            H                   H
            L                   L
            E                   E
            R                   R
```

all over the goal posts.

Children, without knowing anything about him,
spray GUSTAV MAHLER
on to schools.
People begin registering babies with the names GUSTAV MAHLER.

It's the way things take off.
It's the way families break apart.
It's the way people get arrested, tried, convicted, executed.
It's the way dictators come to power.

I didn't want any of this, mumbles Gustav.
And he asks if I could be so kind
as to buy him a glass of whiskey.
Funds, he says, *are a little low.*

As I stand at the bar
people come in from their offices.
One says the words GUSTAV MAHLER
are now attaching themselves to in-house emails.

Another says she looked out of the window
and saw GUSTAV MAHLER
reflected in sunlight on Lake Ontario
Undoing a button of her blouse,
she orders the bar's new GUSTAV MAHLER cocktail.

I turn around with the whiskey
and Gustav's gone.
I go to the door
and catch a glimpse of him
scurrying away
down the crowded sidewalk,
his Blue Jays cap pulled tighter,
his coat collar turned high.
Gustav, I call out. *Gustav.*
Everything's going to be okay.
And I know it's not.

Nelson and Hardy Play Scrabble Before Trafalgar

It's Nelson's turn but he's pondering the last letter
from Emma, its tone of disillusionment, its jagged
uneven handwriting, its subjects the sudden
death of her favourite spaniel, Ned, and the rain.

Hardy drums his fingers on the oak table, tugs
at his necktie, shuffles in his seat.
The lop-sided one that makes his back ache.
Sorry, says Nelson, and hums a tune that
might be *Those In Peril On The Sea*.

Hah! says Nelson and with a flourish lays SNUFFBOX
on a triple word, using an F that's already down
and dropping the S on the end of FLAG.

Nelson eases back in his leather-cushioned chair
rests his thumb in the pocket of his waistcoat
chews on the end of his unlit pipe.

Hardy's hatred wells in his throat.
The day before he'd been winning when
Nelson spread out the word URGH
to win by a single point.
His protests that URGH wasn't a word
drew the slyest of smiles.

Now Hardy stares glumly at his row
of tiles: Three As, three Es and the Q.

The Bet

(A weaver named George Kettering won a 10-guinea bet that he could stand on one leg, with no other support, for four hours. Sporting Magazine, 1820)

I fear not lack of strength but the moment dreams take over.
To stave off sleep I have plastered my hair with foul-smelling oil.
To guard against ease I have put on a shirt of sackcloth.
And I have taken advice.

Melly, the blind mountaineer, said:
Gamblers must see the earth in their hearts.
He also recommended reliving one's life
from the sunlight to the echo.
And after that, he said, *become your father.*

Mortimer, poor man, was of no help.
His one-hundred mile run in circuits of twenty yards
celebrated with such vigour only a few months ago
had left him mad.
The beautiful, he said, *have twenty-eight words for bicycle.*

And so, at six in the evening, in the upstairs room
of Harmer the Pugilist, at the sign of the Plough, I step
into the chalk circle in my ragged shirt, with my gleaming hair
and stand on my strong right leg (left bent back, no hopping).
I welcome the seconds coming in like a line
of fourteen thousand new friends.

The Water Diviner

The thirsty people pay
and crowd to watch, but
for now the trick is in
the drama, in the measure

of the stride, the heavy
dance of the methodical
tread, and in the way
water rises at full moon

to break the boundaries
of grief. My reward is in
coins, a place to rest,
quiet nods of respect.

Sometimes, too, after dark
women will seek me out
for more elusive miracles.
But that is not my craft.

Des

Des used to stand at the end of the bar
in the Cross Guns
on King's Heath High Street
He liked me to pour his lager flat
ate one packet of crisps
one bag of scratchings
a day.

Sometimes if things were quiet
and he wasn't
oiled enough
to sing *Moon River*
or
dance his Matilda Waltz
he'd tell me about
his son in Sydney
a sister in the outback
an ex-wife
who could long jump six metres.

Everybody thought Des was okay.

When he stopped coming in
nobody asked after him
and
I didn't think of him
until now.

Wood

Jack builds a log-shelter in half a day, and from felled firs
and logs dragged from the brook and dried,
a hide with gabled roof.

I'll not forget his woolly-hatted fourteen-year-old beam,
nails in his teeth, in the rain astride a branch,
bow-saw slung across his shoulder.

Rustic bookcases, coffee tables appear
out of old pallets, mushrooms chain-sawed
from forgotten stumps.

Already he works each year with the grain.

Fishing with Jack

at the edge
of the pond
without need
of words
we tie on our hooks

Jack casts his line

I drop in the pole

a dragonfly
on Jack's float.

I toss in
maggots

pour tea
from the flask

wait for
bubbles
and swirls
in the water

it doesn't matter
what happens

Test Paper

What is Aunt Louisa's book about?
What is Item 12 in the centre glass case made of?
Where were the children's shoes found?
If you listen hard enough can you hear the family below?
What was the name of the chair-maker?
What is the black market price for an osprey egg?
Was it Rag, Tag or Bob-Tail who ate the rare orchid?
Why is the new century a concertina of high houses?
When will the accordionist grow wings?
When can a swimming pool be the tongue of a dog?
If you put on skins will you ever take them off?
What does it mean to sing?

Holding the Days

soon
my son
will not
build
shelters
in the woods

will not
marvel
at our
pumpkins
and beans

will not
stand
with me
on quiet
evenings
like this

smelling
the
bonfires
of our
times

Ellyn, Stratford Pool

It's 6.30 a.m.
Her blue costume,
the blue water.
Length after length
an hour non-stop.
The ease she has,
the elegance of it.
On the way back
to egg on toast
and the bus
to school
I ask what
she thinks
when
she's swimming
like that.
Nothing,
she says.
Not a thing.

Campsite

Outside the tent.
Dew on grass.
The sun is already hot.
I drink the first
coffee of the day
decide at low tide
to wade to the old
oyster beds
past Hermit Rock.

Lydia comes
out of the tent
hugs me
checks
the cereal box
for ear-wigs
says, *Dad*
I think today
the sea
will be
apple juice.

On the Famous Photograph of Stanley Matthews on Mount Everest

He took on trust his head for heights
learned in advance how to handle an ice-pick,
for comfort screwed extra-long studs into his best boots,
and for luck took the cap from his England debut
against Wales in nineteen thirty-four.
For inspiration he placed in his pocket the gumshield
of his father, Jack, the Fighting Barber of Hanley.

Tensing couldn't be bothered to go up again,
so sent his brother, who knew by heart the yak-hide map
handed down by their forefathers.
Tensing and his brother always steered guests clear
of the crevasse where Irving lay, made sure to circumvent
Mallory's parched body, sitting upright as if gazing over Tibet.

If they disliked a man it was said
they led him in agonising circles
until he pleaded to be taken down.

Tensing's brother liked Stanley Matthews
and pressed him for football stories:
Was Tom Finney really so down to earth?
Was playing at Wembley that tough on the calves?
Who was better, Mortensen or Lofthouse?

Out of respect Tensing's brother took Stanley up
the easiest way, though did extend the climb
by one night at Base Camp Two
in order to discuss a theory he had
that Hungary would be the next big footballing nation.
It was there, by the way, the famous photo was taken
not at the summit.

And so Stanley strolled nonchalantly out of the clouds
into a hero's welcome in Kathmandu.
He told the world's press he had done it for the young Queen
and, slapping the back of a hung-over hack,
said it had given him something to do in the cricket season.
He joked that if he'd known what a bitter wind
there was at the top, he'd have taken a scarf
and also teased fans he had a blister on his right foot
as big as Blackpool.

The Gallery of Goalkeepers

Once we have paid our admission fee
we are required to jog to one end of the room
wave to banks of virtual fans and
after touching the crossbar of the goal installation
throw cap and gloves into the net.
We have already complained about the cost
of hiring these for such brief, if dramatic, purpose.

When the whistle blows exhibits
are wheeled into position: we can choose
4-2-4, 4-4-2 or 4-3-3.
Other permutations are considered
insufficiently historical. To use
the old 2-3-5 W formation
a special permit has to be applied for
in advance.

As we patrol our penalty area
we see pass before us
Bert Trautmann's neck brace
the stretcher that carried away John Thomson
the diaries, unfortunately not yet translated
from the Russian, of Lev Yashin.
Also, his famous black jersey.
Seaman's pony-tail.
The x-ray of Ray Wood's jaw.
A bootleg of Frank Haffey singing in the bath.
A plaster cast of Banks' right hand bent
at the exact angle required to flick
Pele's header over the bar.
This exhibit is enlarged to fill the whole
of one wall.

Leaning in a corner, forever smiling, is Frank Swift
with his thick eyebrows and jet black hair.
His hand is open where someone has stolen
the copy of the News of the World containing
his last column from February 1958.

Locked for his own safety in a corner cabinet
poor Bonetti, caught at the near post,
and McTavish of East Stirlingshire who sliced
a throw-in into his own net.

Hanging from the central dome of the ceiling
Tomaczewski's legs.

In the bay window Shilton's shadow spreads large.
We are invited to advance into a virtual one-on-one.

Inlaid on a side wall, we can stand against
Eddie Hopkinson, the 5ft 8in miracle.

A label on a red box says: Property of Liverpool FC.
Secret trajectory of the Flying Pig.

And on we go into other more obscure rooms,
the goalkeepers from parks and marshes,
from scrubland and Astroturf,
penalty saves gathered together and filed on microfiche,
in all the languages of the world
landmarks of the lunacy, the sheer nonsensical madness
of the custodians of the globe.

On the way out
we do not argue as
the enormous bulk of Fatty Foulke
guides us towards the museum shop.

Elizabeth Barrett Browning's Lost Years

I knew her well, of course. She was with me
on the occasion of the Gettysburg Address.
It was a Thursday, I believe. I wouldn't say
she had any real influence on it, but against
that she was never content with making the
sandwiches. She teased Lincoln, who was
slightly deaf, by miming at the dinner table.

Her marriage didn't last. Robert took off when
they reached Florence. She wrote *Aurora Leigh*
while considering the technicalities, then
took a steamer to Iceland. On board
she tried to teach the Transylvanian crew
the subtleties of cricket. I know from
experience she had a vicious under-arm
top-spinner. The game ended when
she heaved a long hop into the North Sea.

She slipped into New York just before
the end of the war. By then she had spent
too long with her Icelandic goatherd by
a lake where midges went to die. The
earth formations spiralled out of the water,
she said. Her hands were a little shaky
but you could tell it was her from
the portraits. She had that
gravelly voice too. When the war
was done and we had to work out what
was best, I took her to Gettysburg
for the company. These things can be
awfully stuffy. She had no time for Everett,
who she called a bloody windbag, and
thought Nicolay and Hay unkind,
spiteful little men. Surreptitiously,

I believe she did a little editing while their backs were turned.
We lost touch after that, but she did send a postcard from India. She was travelling, she said, to the end of the line with a railway clerk she had met in Lucknow and was, as usual, in dire need of funds. I did not reply.

Mr and Mrs Shakespeare in a Café in Rother Street

He buys Oxford University sweat-shirts cheap
and is pleased.
He sits with Ann, who writes postcards
and sips peppermint tea.
It's raining.
Ann feels she might have a slight chill,
shudders at how little young girls wear these days.
William strokes the back of her hand
then takes out
from a British Home Stores carrier bag
a pack of three babygros
he got in the summer sales.
William smiles, says
Do you think they will be pleased?
Ann says they will. She's sure they will.
His bacon sandwich arrives, with a sprig of parsley
and a grape.
He frowns, pokes the grape with his forefinger,
flicks off the parsley
asks the waitress
for brown sauce.

Camping, Northern Spain

I finish the Rioja
watch lightning over hills
wonder if it would be
a good time to walk
on the beach.

I pick up a book.
Chasing Saturday Night
by Michael Kriesel.

In a caravan
an argument
erupts
in English.
He shouts *Yes!*
She shouts *No!*

A muffled
thud.

An owl
in the distance.

Waves
on the shingle.

Before

I did a crossword and found your name in it
and dreamed of what we were
before mountain goats were clambering
up and down the slopes of my word bag
and making a hell of a noise
before you tired of my attempts to ask
the world why Marlene Dietrich
seemed taller than five-feet-two
and Adolf Hitler
seemed shorter than five-feet-nine
before you tired of my insistence that
The Rolling Stones really did play
a children's party at Nuneaton Co-Op
Social Club and were pelted with buns,
before dear old dad repeated
the family stories in the green arm chair
by the log fire
before that pub in Harlow in '71
where a woman played
For The Benefit Of Mister Kite
in whatever key was to hand
before we witnessed the massed ukuleles
of the George Formby Appreciation Society
playing *Leaning On A Lampost*
on a foggy night
in Leamington Spa
before the tourists took photos
of the girl who fell through
the earth's crust and screamed for help
as she blundered around in boiling mud
before John Frith threw a rock
at King George The Third

before I wanted you or you wanted me
before Man Ray photographed Lee Miller
before you photographed me
standing on the ruins
looking out to sea
at whatever might be there

Vigil

It's the stormy season.

The police
are mostly interested
in keeping dry
and I cross
a country for you.

Here's the wire.

Here's everything
they would
have us be.

I can't send words
on desire
on kindness
on distance
or the lack of it.

When happiness
bounces off
the dead
I might as well
bring
chamber music

the world on
black paper

asbestos as art.

In the rain
I cross
the bridge
peer into
the dark
and wait.

I don't know
what good
it will do
but
here's the wire,
here's everything
we are.

Stranded

Needing a break
from observation
notification
classification
he rests his eyes
takes a square
of protein from
his anorak pocket
remembers coffee
how good it tasted
after a journey.

He looks out
across the ice
at tall bleak firs far off
sees ancient
comforting oaks
feels a breeze
always a warm breeze
stops short of
a hammock
strung between elms
whole lifetimes of leaves
moving under the sun.

He hears languages
float in with the blizzard
words, phrases, poems
merge from birdsong
into French
from Ancient Norse
into the purring of a cat

from Something by
The Beatles
into that piece
by Sibelius
that always
opens
The Sky at Night.

He pulls his sealskins
tighter
waits for winter
or the storm
or whatever
it turns out to be
to pass.

A Hat

I come home from the back fields
open the red front door
go to hang my coat on the peg in the hallway
and see a hat already hanging there.
A woman's felt hat.

I take it down. It's round, would fit snugly.
I don't recognise its swirling colours.

I go quietly into the kitchen.
Nobody's there, except the cat asleep
on the cushion by the stove.

I go from room to room
switch on lights, call out
Is anyone here?

I go back to the hallway.
Put the hat back on the peg.

A Giant

Nothing has happened yet but
in the dark room at the top of the stairs
two lovers roll among the coats on a single bed.

Nothing will happen until
the oak tree on top of the hill
becomes a hat
as out of the earth beneath it
a giant rises.

Then as the earth rumbles and thunders
the lovers will stop fumbling
will sit bolt upright
to listen and wonder
what terror
is to be released upon the world.

But it will be okay, really it will.

The giant will already be
climbing slowly into the swirling sky
holding on to her new hat.

Not Leaving

The past shifts uneasily
at the back of the drawer,
moves soundlessly
into the room where
the family gathers
at night.

I hear the ripples
from the small hymns
of conversation in
dreams and the intricate
gambles that make
our living hours
what they are.

You will know
I am here.

Beach Cricket

A nun has joined in a game of beach cricket
with lads in baseball caps
and England football shirts
and bright tattoos.

She's fielding in the sea
her grey habit tucked into her expansive drawers.
Her laughter floats out across the waves.

It should reach Holland by nightfall.

Walking Across the Mersey

On the third Sunday of the month at low tide
members of the Society of Tall Persons walk across the Mersey.

After assembling at an undisclosed address in Birkenhead
they file quietly through terraced streets
in bathing hats, trunks and, in case of emergency, snorkels.

After a brief speech by the chairman
and the singing of the society song
there is a compulsory period of limbering up
under the gaze of the official masseur,
who patrols the lines in white flannels
and ceremonial sweater spun from Cumbrian wool.
He is, by tradition, last into the water.

The society admits no responsibility in the event of a casualty
though occasional losses are considered unavoidable.
One man, listening to a Tremeloes' CD on his iPod
failed to hear the warning siren, drifted too far left
and had to be winched clear of shipping lanes
by the coastguard. Members still speak in awe of the sight
of him flapping in the net like a giant squid.

After the Diamond Jubilee crossing in '84
was televised by BBC Southport and rebroadcast
across the world, international visitors began to arrive,
including the hirsute Ukrainian basketball player who
set a record time which is expected to last into the next century.
One family, believed Mongolian, arrived at Lime Street
with a 7ft 2in daughter in national costume.
When she was stripped and greased, she stood at the water's edge,
as her father circled her, clapping his hands and beaming.

An old lady the society records presume was her grandmother
sprinkled her with dust from an ancient stone pot.
It is said the girl, who was expected to find a suitor, spent
the crossing deep in prayer. She was also badly bitten by midges.

Since the dredging of the river in '89, at the deepest point
there is often only a row of heads and shoulders visible.
(The dredging caused an emergency meeting
of the society committee and led, following a test walk,
to a minimum restriction of 6ft 6 1/4in, the height incidentally,
of the former heavyweight champion Jess Willard,
who was very briefly a member between the wars
until an unseemly incident in the Adelphi involving a chambermaid
and an aspidistra caused his card to be withdrawn.)

It is not unusual for the crossing to attract crowds who,
after camping out overnight, binoculared, line the dock.
Usually there is applause as the procession rises from the water,
an image that can appear ghostly if there is a sea-fret,
which has led some inexperienced observers
to lend undue religious significance to the occasion.

Once the stragglers have been helped ashore and offered
a choice of cordials or, in the event of severe cold,
a vintage port from Cadiz, a crate of which is said
to have been a gift from one of the Dukes of York,
a circle is formed, the society song sung,
and a toast drunk to absent friends. De-greased,
invigorated, members take their leave with merry waves.

It is not unusual for the society to be flooded by letters
of appreciation, all of which receive polite replies,
though, since the unfortunate death of the short man who,
unspotted by the committee, attempted to cross on stilts,
approaches for media interviews, especially from
The Liverpool Post & Echo, have been discouraged.

Grief

In the morning
on a bench
in a park
by a pool
a couple
smoking.

The man
sunglasses
on top
of his
shaven
head
reads *La
Repubblica*.

The woman
plump with
red shoes
pushes
back
and
forth
with one
hand
an empty
pram.

Rain

What happens when your wife changes her number?

The man worries, even in dreams, wakes into wind-chimes,
a gong, the ghost of a piano. No, there is a piano.
We leave notes.

In the north inflatables have replaced cars
and lifeboats patrol the streets.
Looters are out and about.
The Prime Minister is to address us on television.

In the storm a blackbird flies into the man's house,
slams into the metal chimney over the fire
and falls to the floor.
The man throws a towel over it, carries it out to the lawn.

He looks over to the green bench beneath the birches
where the wind whistles and roars, where once
he and his wife talked for hours.

Rain hurls itself out of the sky.

Where Things Go

The indicator on the oast house is on the move.
Storms are coming in from the south.
The ivy knows it, fastens itself tighter to the wall.
The rotten log knows it, burrows into its hollow beneath the apple tree.
The cockerel, pigeons, blackbirds, they all know it.
Before the rain comes, I'll walk through the wheat in the wind.
See where the footpath goes. Then I'll go in, shut the doors,
Pour a beer. Wait for it to begin and eventually go, the way things do.

Early Morning, Herefordshire

A white-haired man
wheels a wooden barrow
across a lane to a pile of logs.

A black sheep-dog
pushes itself after him.

A cockerel on a gate-post
shines in the sun.

Of Gambling and Poetry

The poet has come from Canada.
He's nervous, stumbles his lines, has the shadow of a stammer.
His booming wife, in the front row, either gives him confidence
or takes it away.
I enjoy his poems about life on the edge of a lake,
sense he's not sure why he's agreed to make the trip
but now he has is settling down.
Perhaps might even enjoy it.

The old man in front of me, dozing, begins to whistle.
A cough travels along our row, stops at the woman next to me.
Convulsed by the effort to repress it,
she scrabbles in her bag, unwraps a mint humbug.

The poet reads a poem about Joni Mitchell.
The one after that is about sitting in a boat, fishing.
Another about deciding not to take a bus.
His wife interrupts, laughs:
You've never taken a bloody bus in your life!
We are embarrassed.
The poet stutters through his next poem.
The reading is cut short by a man starting up
his lawnmower outside the window.
The poet beams as he receives his specially inscribed bowl.

I buy his book, don't bother
with the queue for the signature,
go to the bookies around the corner.
It's South African racing and dogs at Romford and Catford.
A horse misses out but two dogs come up
and I put a mad twenty at three to one
on a seventeen-year-old kid called Sharapova
to win the Wimbledon women's final.

And for the hell of it have five each way
on something called Ice Age at sixteens at Turfontein.
It plays up in the stalls, is last at halfway,
then bolts up like a mad thing to beat the even money jolly
by a length. I'm a hundred to the good
and Sharapova's just warming up.

I eat fish and chips, sit in the sun,
try two poets called Jacob and Chloe
who don't get to me no matter how hard I try.
When I come out, I put my head into the bookies
and Sharapova, bless her blonde pony-tail,
is holding up the winner's trophy.

It's a fine day that might go on getting better.
There's a Bulgarian poet on at four o'clock.
Adrian Mitchell tonight.

The Open Mic Poetry Reading

There is a bare 60 watt bulb in the centre of the ceiling. The landlord has not considered it necessary to light the fire. He stands behind the bar, bald and shining, offering beer with menaces.

The host is Dave. He begins with a brief welcome, a regret that numbers are down tonight, then reads to the end of his nose an informally arranged sonnet about a man who marries the same woman twice. (Dave, it is well known, has done this himself.)

Then a woman in a skimpy dress introduces herself in what might be a Russian accent. She tells us she confines herself to odes on the subjects of Princess Diana and the Euro. After 14 poems, or perhaps one long poem that appears to end 14 times, Dave asks her to have another go later on. She scowls, flounces out, spitting: *But I have ten more yet!*

Next up is a woman who looks as if she steals children's footballs and refuses to give them back. She smells like an oil spill. She reads rhymes about relationships and how hers never work out.

Then a woman demands, before she reads, a table to be provided. She places on it a cup and saucer, then reads, from a piece of paper which she turns in a circle, about a cup and saucer. Next she tells us, apparently ad-libbing, a story about a man named Bill, who moved in with her and moved out, and a cat, also named Bill, who moved in and didn't move out.

When I wake up, it's the turn of a couple who between them cradle bagpipes. As they arrange themselves around the microphone and amplifier they have brought with them, the landlord clatters and swears as he pours Dave a half-pint of mild. This is the first drink he has sold so far.

The bagpipe man explains he is learning the instrument. This is obvious, not only because of the flexibility of the arrangement of the old air from the porridge advert, but because his partner has to help, as he plays the pipes, by squeezing the bag. The result is disturbing.

I buy a beer. It tastes of soap. I do not complain.

Then the late-comer shuffles through the door in a stained Glastonbury '85 T-shirt. He has bubbles of saliva at the corners of his mouth, owl-like spectacles, and carries a Greenpeace carrier bag stuffed with sheets of paper. He tells us of his life-long fascination with buses and, more specifically, bus-routes, and also with the life and works of Samuel Johnson. His poem is about a bus going around a roundabout. Or, as it has several verses, several roundabouts. Or several buses going around several roundabouts. He waves what appears to be an over-exposed photograph of a bus as an illustration. His poem ends with a punchy lament on the inconvenience caused by the temporary closure of the bus station cafe, where it is his habit to read Rasselas.

He thanks us for listening and leaves.

Dave asks brightly if the couple with the bagpipes would like another try. They would. During the clatter and confusion of setting up, I feign a coughing fit, wave an apology and stumble out. As I walk down the road I hear them strike up a not-altogether similar version of the porridge oats tune.

An old man leans in his doorway, looks up at the pub window, flicks cigarette ash into a bush.

Las Vegas, 6.15 a.m.

From the window
of my room
on the twenty-eighth floor
I see a woman
in a pool
her black costume
her mesmeric
breaststroke.
Sunglasses
on a white table.
A towel slung
over a chair.

I go to fetch coffee
from the stall
by the casino.
People scream and
whoop it up at
another jackpot
that won't change
anything.

Back in the room
I pull a chair
to the desk
settle to write
wonder
how it is
I keep
getting paid
to do this
and what
it is
exactly
that I do.

Sunlight on
hoardings
big as houses
advertise
Celine Dion
Mama Mia
The Titanic
Exhibition.

A drifting
blur of
brake lights
stretches
into the
red desert
where
mountains
soften
against
the yellow
sky, and
planes
come
and go
over
Sonny
Liston's
grave.

In the Hotel Room Next to the Mountain

To find me, you turn left at the salivating vulture, don't hesitate
when the mules begin to talk, go up the escalator on the north face
and follow the signs to where the one-legged beggar
recites the lyrics of *Help Me, Rhondda*. It's hard to breathe up here.
Give him your change, for change you will.

I can't even begin to list whatever it is that makes us mad
or lost, or last in line. (You went to Peru and always could
paint better than me. Especially arms, I can't do arms.)
I thought I knew the difference between chance and luck
(I did, I did) until you smiled and squeezed my hand.

Outside it looks like a war zone but it's only the next mountain
being demolished. The beep-beep-beep
of reversing lorries is unbelievably irritating.
The great wrecking-ball slams into grass, earth, rock.

Nobody told September the 29th 2007 its time was nearly up.
I hear it squealing, see its tears showering down.
Very soon I won't be here, won't feel on my bare arm
the soft fabric of this uncomfortable armchair.

I look at the salt-spray and rain and splashes of cement
on the window. It must be twenty years since I lay on a bed
in a room just like this and heard guns way below in the street.
Now I think on the terrible baying of terrified mules
falling off the cliff path that cracks and crumbles.

The telephone rings. It's you. Let's meet again, I say,
let's take the coast road, have lunch somewhere, perhaps
where the waitress is kind and honest and unaffected
and people are going about their lives and there is a sea view.

The battery died on your laptop in Peru, you say.
Then you call the movie *The Motorcycle Diaries*
a must-have event, ask if I saw one of the Beach Boys
on Seinfeld. I'm sorry, I say,
I don't know what Seinfeld is but I do know
juniper berries are really good with venison
and it's chaos for genealogists before
the Lord Hardwicke Marriage Act of 1754.
You say we should leave the past where it is
and hang up.

The vulture flaps about beyond the window
its saliva stringing out on the breeze.

Clearing the Boundaries of the Revolution

We use sickles, machetes. Row by row
we sing the songs of the revolution.
Yes, of course, there are rumours behind walls

murmurs behind hands. Our son speaks of vague
whispers of a plague of voles in the south.
My wife and I, we do not believe this.

However, for the national good in
case of emergency, I have begun
the systematic trapping of weasels.

The Ice

Our friends wave us off from the quay, peer
through the rain—the pastor, too, his oilskin
buttoned at the neck.
I know they consider us mad.
We strain for the last glimpse
of their lanterns.

Journeys become purges.
When the wind howls in the rigging
none of us is without crisis.
Even on the darkest nights you can see
the green eyes of the dogs
we tether on the deck.

By October, we are encased in ice
We run the dogs, our sleds
fast as falling stars. Borovski somehow
takes down a reindeer
with his lassoo.
Then winter closes in.
Sleep comes as we stand.
My wife's hand, is it? On the edge
of my collar, smoothing my hair.
Or dead Franklin warning us off.

The only possible cause for the instability
of the compass is iron in the strange hills
that one moment are there, and the next
are no more than clouds. On an iceberg
far to the north we see Franklin's ship
pass as if chained to the sky.

Smoke from the lamps weaves swirls
in the fog. When I stare into it, guilt
throbs and pounds behind my temples.
The Arctic is no place for tired men
and Franklin is back, his lank hair
flapping on his frozen skull.

The next morning the sun is out
it's calm and I see Inuit children
playing football. It seems to me
the girls are the better players.

And we find a rhythm in running
aground and grinding and rocking,
swaying and dipping our way off again,
the dead roar of reef and rock, then just
floating and lapping.

The night the propeller breaks we lose DuPont.
What makes him, of all of us, slip from the rigging?
We bury him on a hill beneath a cross of rock
overlooking the sound. My tears turn white.
Our bones press in on us.

We believe the ice wants to take us north,
but in the spring it sings a brighter song.
We are travelling south-west,
past bears trapped on loose floes
floating clear into a blue sea.

And then one April night we see the lamps
of a small steamer, and far in the distance
more lights, and more, bigger and brighter.

Before we know it a foghorn welcomes us in
and on the quay in their thousands they stand.
Men remove their caps and sing
in a hundred languages,
the women's voices joining in,
rising above them like waves.

House of Fun

When they renovated the house
they went from room to room
burying laughter behind walls, deep
below floorboards.

I hear it most in the kitchen
on summer nights like this
when the ghost of a cook
peels spuds at the long table
and her sometime lover
the ghost of a scullery maid
recently arrived from Northumberland
paints her nails the colour of seals.

As the sky clears into dawn
I hear their laughter
trailing off
into the smell of lilacs.

Dreaming on the Broken Boulevard

Bogart and Dean are at the bar, drinking bourbon, talking possibility.
Monroe walks in like the letter S, orders Pepsi.
Elvis serves her, says: *How's your mother, Marilyn?*
She rasps: *Oh, you know,* toys with the jukebox.

Bogart stubs his Craven A in the Welcome to Wisconsin ashtray
says: *I've gotta cut down.*
Dean tells him: *Someday I'll drive a Porsche.*

Elvis breathes on a glass, polishes it, listens as
Basilio and Robinson get it on in the Garden.
Elvis whistles Hound Dog under his breath
Says, *That Syracuse onion-picker's giving him hell.*

The house of cards Bogart's built on the bar collapses.
He drains his glass with loving care.
Dean turns to watch Marilyn sway as she loses herself
in *How Much Is That Doggy In The Window?*

Utopia, California, 1999

There was a hippo in my room. I had everything I needed: a bed, a fridge, table and chairs, racks for food and cups. Electricity. I'd come in from work, put down my tools, take a beer from the fridge, eat and think and watch and listen. And I admit after a while the hippo got to be company. Okay it wasn't a really big one, but it was a hippo—every so often it sighed, raised its head and yawned, and looked at me as I moved around it. The hippo, I should say now, was bright red, as if somebody had painted it for a circus act.

In the middle of the hottest summer I could remember, it rained. Enough rain to fill a desert, to end a famine. At that the hippo lugged itself over to the window and sat there, gazing out through the streaked dirty glass into the smog-and-rain sky. I ate my meal at the table and said nothing. When the rain stopped the hippo went back to the middle of the room, lay down and went to sleep.

Anyway, I was thinking of moving out. There was a place across the road but it was upstairs and open-plan. That is, it didn't have a wall at the front so you just existed above the street. There was a back wall, and it was split level, so you could live nicely towards the back and not be disturbed but have all the light that was going. To get to it you had to pass Skid or his wife Alma, who sat down at the front door. Alma had been a dare-devil rider on the Wall of Death at the circus. *I could do it all,* she said. *Handstands, no hands, read a newspaper, drink a cup of coffee. I wore red boots, a red coat with gold tasselled epaulets and a tall hat with red pom-poms. Somebody said I looked like Ava Gardner, but I don't think she was much to look at.*

They had the ground floor and didn't really want anybody living above them, or so I was told. But they didn't own the place. Nobody did. So I thought about moving there. Of course I wondered about the hippo. If it would come with me. If it did, what would people do about it? Nobody had seen it before. And I hadn't said anything about it, not even to Mack, who I worked next to in the line. We didn't like each other but sometimes we said a few words. I think he had a wife who pretty much stayed wherever it was he lived. Or maybe he didn't. I don't know. He talked about her anyway.

The new place had yellow walls like out of a Mexican movie. I still wasn't sure whether or not I had moved in. Skid and Alma weren't very nice people but who is, what's the difference, they weren't killers or anything. And they got used to me and most of the time we didn't say anything to each other. Skid played a blues harmonica and rode a 1936 Flathead and Alma cooked dinners that smelled bitter and hot. Finally, when I stopped going back to the old place I realised I had definitely moved out. I don't know what happened to the hippo. It might still be there.

Now I sit at the back of my open plan yellow room and do what I do. I come in from work, put my tool-bag by the door, take a cold beer from the fridge and think. The vile smell of Alma's cooking wafts up. Tonight Skid's put on a blues record, an old LP from the good days. It's better than listening to his harmonica.

It's so hot I need to lie down, so I do. I can't be bothered to cook tonight. Alma's put me off it. Now I hear her talking on the telephone. I didn't know they had a telephone. The trouble with telephones, I guess, is that when they ring, it's the sign that somebody else wants to talk to you, so you have to be pretty mean or anti-social not to talk back. I'm glad I don't have a telephone. I'm beginning to think I need a front wall to keep out the traffic noise and the car fumes that sometimes coil up in the heat and gather here. Maybe I could build one. Then again I don't know anything about the strength of walls. Maybe there used to be a wall to this room and it fell down and maybe if I built a new one that would fall down too. It could kill someone.

Perhaps it's just time to move on. I could call in at the old place before I leave just to say hello again and goodbye. Perhaps see if the hippo's all right or if there's somebody else there now. Anyway, I don't really need the job anymore and the century's about to end, the whole millennium's going to be done with forever. Maybe I'll go south. At the weekend. Yes, the weekend. South. That'll do it. South.

Ericsson the Engineer in Marshalsea Jail

I have dreams so vivid that I toss and turn on my steel bed.
Sometimes I wake when my face touches the damp walls.

One day there will be railways under seas, over mountains
and through them. The sound of steam trains will
enrich our imaginations, stations will be built
that will glorify our sense of adventure.

The food, by the way, is so bad I believe they mean to kill us.
I despair I shall never get out, but as a great man once said
Despair I can handle, it's hope that will finish me off.

And what sort of a country is this that will jail a sane man
for such a paltry misdemeanour as debt?

I admit I got it wrong with the passenger train
but it was my first try. It was not fully refined.
Even so, had I been English they would have given me time.
I could have re-positioned the boiler, increased
the capacity of the bellows.

And I still believe in the prototype
for the Monitor Turret Battleship.
It's entirely practical, if a little immoral.
An American is coming to see me about it
thinks it may be of interest to them
in their forthcoming war.
I hope he has the wherewithal
to pay in advance.

The Guardians of the Lady's Slipper Orchid

On the porch of their hut
they finished the last bottle of Sicilian red.
After that, it was grappa.
On Sicilian red they discussed poetry,
women, history.
On grappa they fell out
about the implications of the shortage of honey bees
the correct tune for *Beans And Fatback* by Link Wray
the scent wafting up from the meadows.
Burkinshaw thumped his fist on the rickety table,
bellowed: *It's chives, I tell you!*
Crabtree hushed him. They peered nervously
into the valley, knowing without looking
what the other was thinking.
What was that faint, mechanical noise?
That echo?
Was that glint of sunlight
beyond the oak tree
a cowbell
or a camera?

The Release of the First Starlings in America

He's that kind of boss, and that's the fun of it.
You don't know what each day might bring.

I met the boat in: the usual drifters, grifters
and women dragging gaggles of thin kids,
all of them straining for a wave or smile
from a man who had come on ahead.
I don't know what they dream might be here.
And kisses and hugs and broken-toothed grins
all manner of pretties and uglies, and
huddled together those who found nobody,
gathering themselves in.

So I loaded the crates on the cart: four,
twenty-five birds to each.
I did spot one of them, mean-headed thing
with a quizzical eye, but their fate wasn't my worry.
And no point in encouraging the horse
into anything approaching a rush.
The usual chaos in Hell's Kitchen but nothing
I'm not used to, then peaceful enough.

At the Park, the master pacing about, chain-smoking
dodging promenading couples and sellers of tat.
When he saw me he rushed over, grinning,
gesticulating, as if greeting a guest.
I pulled up, as instructed, at the fountain.
He was clapping his hands, gabbling on to some old
Mr Big in a fine hat, something about
introducing to America every bird mentioned
by Shakespeare.

They had a delve into the crates, pulled out
a dead, half-eaten one here and there, tutted
and fussed, picked the live ones up one by one,
turned them over, stroked their heads and wings,
never raised their voices over a whisper, bathed
them in the fountain, then put them back.

I had to put seeds in every cage.
A right squabble that caused.
Then the master did more hand-clapping
and striding about, even offered me one
of his weak rich man's smokes, which was a first.
I thankee'd him, put it behind my ear.

He went quiet and still, then said to let them go.
So I opened the tops of the crates and it was like
an explosion of shrieking, like sunlight on oil, a shape
of shadows in the sky, the sound of the sucking down
of all that fresh American air, and not really a song
but a tide rushing up out of all those tiny throats.
We watched them turn west, becomes dots, like
clever folks' words on a page, then not even that.

Afterwards the breeze, the two of them, and me,
all standing still, the horses snorting and shuffling.
Then the master and his friend walked off
without a word, heads bowed;
left me to go home in my own time.

Wall

It takes time to build a backbone for an island
and what did we divide, aside
from east and west?
Or did we abandon, not finish?
Was another planned to cut north from south
to present to the heavens the sign of a cross?

Perhaps, but our faith encouraged devotion
not questions. And by the end
there were just the four of us,
and we had long forgotten why we'd come,
though the youngest said once
as we watched the sun rise above the sea
he remembered a quest for a notion
half-understood; and somehow stayed.
The wall, should you visit, offers no clue.

Some years it rained for weeks, turned paths
into rutted bogs that froze. I still hear
our sandaled feet and cartwheels crack
the ice, see our rough hands caress
the reliable stones. In glowing autumn mists
and through the slow days of summer
we rolled and lifted them into place;
took the strain in turn for spring after spring.
Our backs, our hearts would burn.

And there were times when blizzards came
and snow drifted deep, and in the sanctuary
of our cells we wondered how much
a winter could undo.

That afternoon when the last stone settled
easily against the rest, we did not
shake hands, break open wine,
give thanks to God, but quietly packed
our tools, retraced our steps, gazed
as we went on how clean, how bright
and strong a line of stone we'd laid.

There is a time for leaving
but what goes, how much stays?
What is it in us that asks no questions
but builds and builds? I didn't know then,
don't know now.

Aunt Mary

I bought Aunt Mary on the Shopping Channel yesterday.

I thought she'd died years ago
but the presenter in the powder-blue suit
and Homer Simpson tie
said she'd been found in
the folds of the dark green sofa
when the home for the blind
was knocked down.

Even after all these years
the moment the remote stalled on channel 666
and item 13
I knew it was Aunt Mary.

Aunt Mary liked flat shoes, coats that buttoned to the neck, plain hats.
Aunt Mary had a Desperate Dan chin (with stubble).
Aunt Mary read leather-bound books in Braille,
       had the top of a finger missing.
Aunt Mary was so appalled by the thought of the act of sex
       she refused the company of men.
Aunt Mary had amazingly green eyes.
Aunt Mary ate Gadsby's Hymns for breakfast,
Sturgeon's Sermons for dinner,
       had a voice that shone like pearls in moonlight.
Aunt Mary's relationship with her father was unclear.

Today Aunt Mary
arrived in an express delivery van
in a large cardboard box.

I've not opened it yet.